Teaching Little Fingers to Play More Children's Song

Piano Solos with Optional Teacher Accompaniments
Arranged by
Carolyn Miller

CONTENTS

Book
ISBN 978-1-4234-6757-1

Book/CD
ISBN 978-1-4234-6758-8

WILLIS MUSIC

EXCLUSIVELY DISTRIBUTED BY

HAL•LEONARD® CORPORATION
7777 W. BLUEMOUND RD. P.O. BOX 13819 MILWAUKEE, WI 53213

Visit Hal Leonard Online at
www.halleonard.com

Supercalifragilisticexpialidocious

from Walt Disney's MARY POPPINS

Optional Teacher Accompaniment

Words and Music by Richard M. Sherman
and Robert B. Sherman
Arranged by Carolyn Miller

Brightly

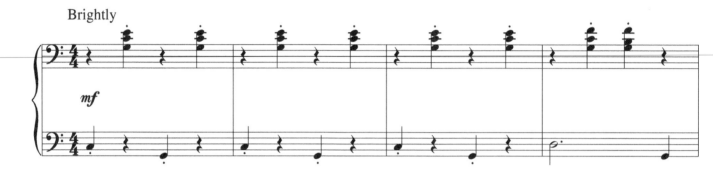

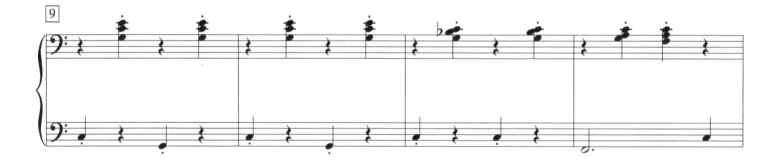

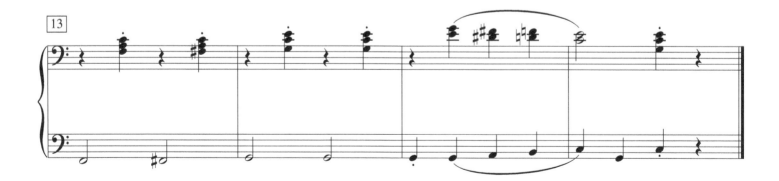

Supercalifragilisticexpialidocious

from Walt Disney's MARY POPPINS

Words and Music by Richard M. Sherman
and Robert B. Sherman
Arranged by Carolyn Miller

Play both hands one octave higher when performing as a duet.

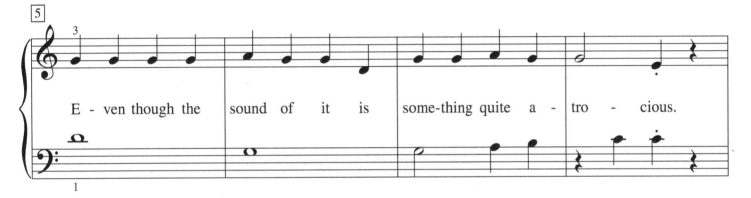

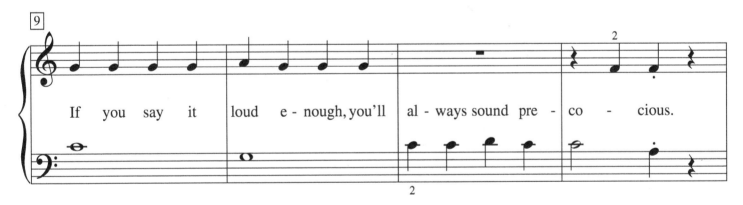

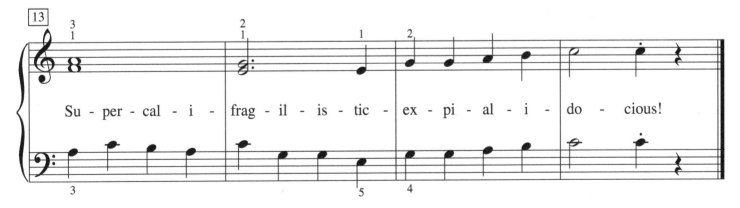

I'm Popeye the Sailor Man

Theme from the Paramount Cartoon POPEYE THE SAILOR

Optional Teacher Accompaniment

Words and Music by Sammy Lerner
Arranged by Carolyn Miller

With energy

I'm Popeye the Sailor Man
Theme from the Paramount Cartoon POPEYE THE SAILOR

Words and Music by Sammy Lerner
Arranged by Carolyn Miller

Play both hands one octave higher when performing as a duet.

With energy

It's a Small World

from "it's a small world" at Disneyland Park and Magic Kingdom Park

Optional Teacher Accompaniment

Words and Music by Richard M. Sherman
and Robert B. Sherman
Arranged by Carolyn Miller

It's a Small World

from "it's a small world" at Disneyland Park and Magic Kingdom Park

Words and Music by Richard M. Sherman
and Robert B. Sherman
Arranged by Carolyn Miller

Play both hands one octave higher when performing as a duet.

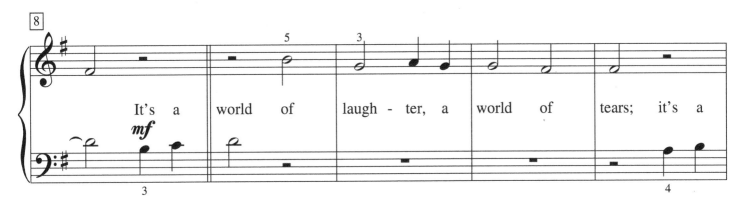

It's a world of laugh - ter, a world of tears; it's a

world of hopes and a world of fears. There's so

Optional Teacher Accompaniment

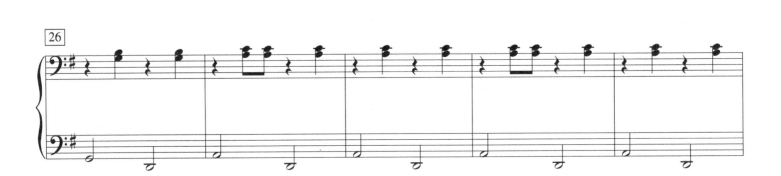

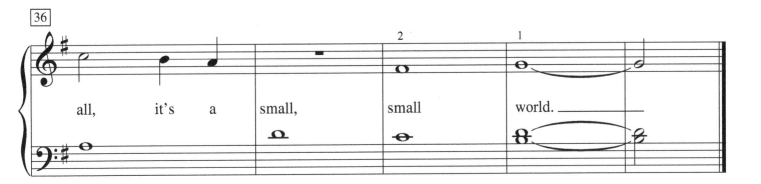

Do-Re-Mi

from THE SOUND OF MUSIC
Optional Teacher Accompaniment

Lyrics by Oscar Hammerstein II
Music by Richard Rodgers
Arranged by Carolyn Miller

With spirit

Do-Re-Mi
from THE SOUND OF MUSIC

Lyrics by Oscar Hammerstein II
Music by Richard Rodgers
Arranged by Carolyn Miller

Play both hands one octave higher when performing as a duet.

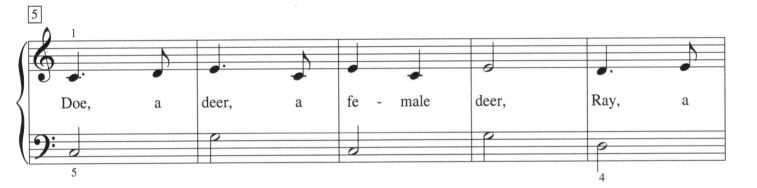

12

Optional Teacher Accompaniment

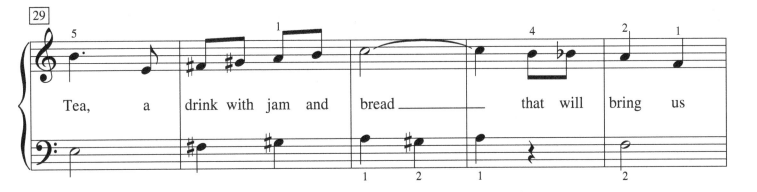

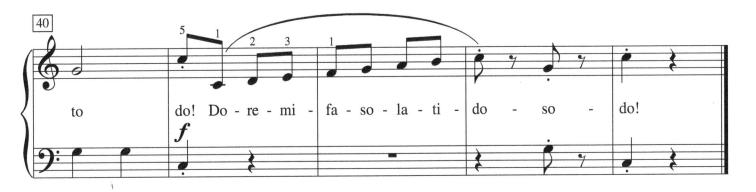

My Favorite Things

from THE SOUND OF MUSIC

Optional Teacher Accompaniment

Lyrics by Oscar Hammerstein II
Music by Richard Rodgers
Arranged by Carolyn Miller

Like a Waltz

My Favorite Things

from THE SOUND OF MUSIC

Lyrics by Oscar Hammerstein II
Music by Richard Rodgers
Arranged by Carolyn Miller

Play both hands one octave higher when performing as a duet.

Like a Waltz

Optional Teacher Accompaniment

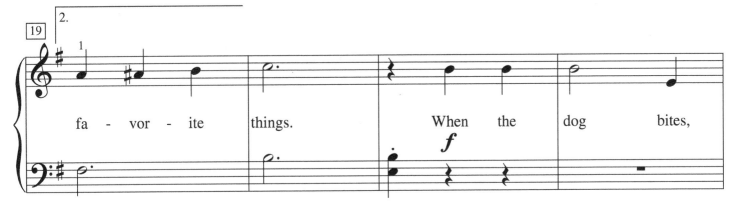

Tomorrow
from the Musical Production ANNIE

Optional Teacher Accompaniment

Lyric by Martin Charnin
Music by Charles Strouse
Arranged by Carolyn Miller

Tomorrow
from the Musical Production ANNIE

Lyric by Martin Charnin
Music by Charles Strouse
Arranged by Carolyn Miller

Play both hands one octave higher when performing as a duet.

Optional Teacher Accompaniment

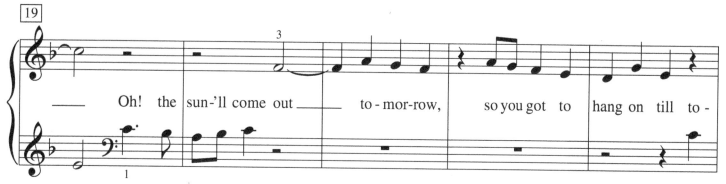

Oh! the sun-'ll come out ___ to-mor-row, so you got to hang on till to-

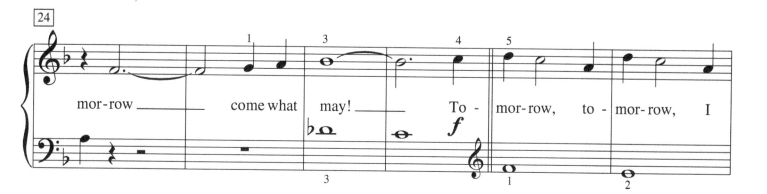

mor-row ___ come what may! ___ To - mor-row, to - mor-row, I

love ya to - mor-row, you're on-ly a day a - way! ___ To -

mor-row, to - mor-row, I love ya to - mor-row, you're on - ly a

day a - way!

The Candy Man

from WILLY WONKA AND THE CHOCOLATE FACTORY

Optional Teacher Accompaniment

Words and Music by Leslie Bricusse
and Anthony Newley
Arranged by Carolyn Miller

The Candy Man

from WILLY WONKA AND THE CHOCOLATE FACTORY

Words and Music by Leslie Bricusse
and Anthony Newley
Arranged by Carolyn Miller

Play both hands one octave higher when performing as a duet.

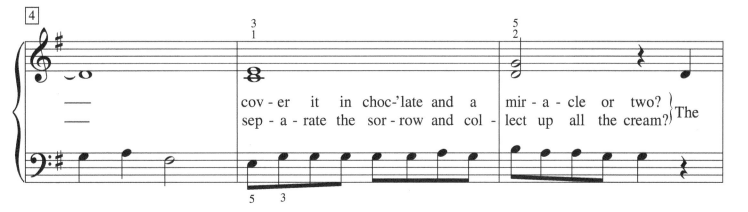

Who can take a sun - rise sprin - kle it with dew,
Who can take to - mor - row dip it in a dream,

cov - er it in choc-'late and a mir - a - cle or two? The
sep - a - rate the sor - row and col - lect up all the cream? The

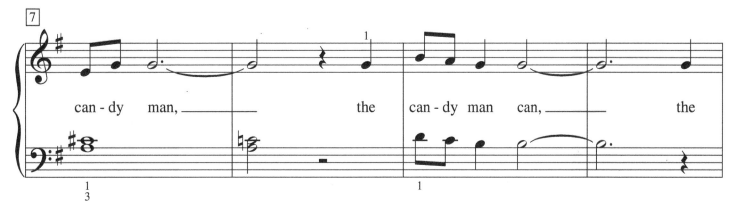

can - dy man, the can - dy man can, the

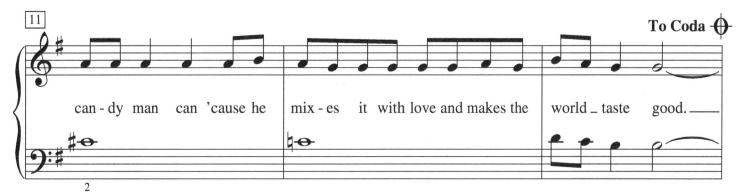

can - dy man can 'cause he mix - es it with love and makes the world taste good.

To Coda ⊕

Optional Teacher Accompaniment

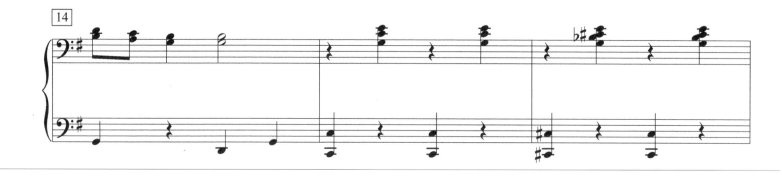

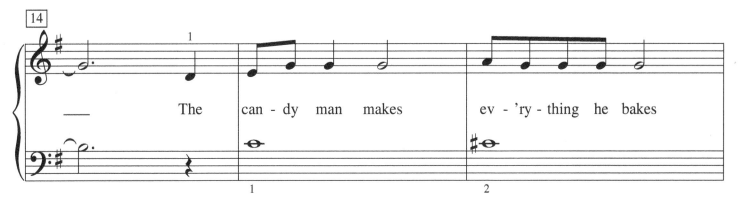

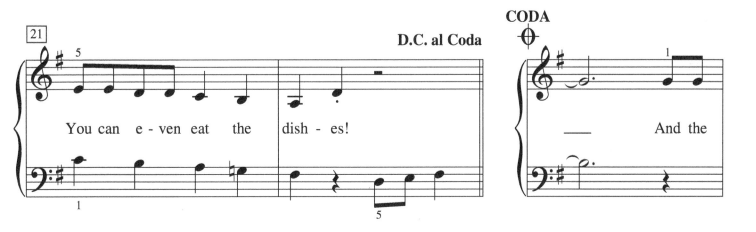

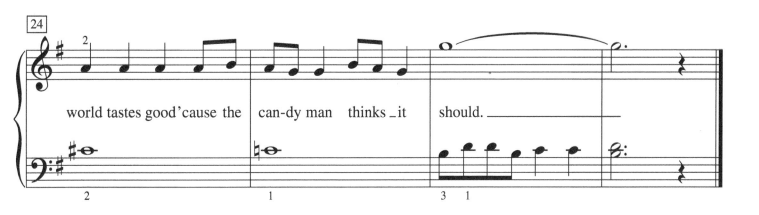

Linus and Lucy

Optional Teacher Accompaniment

By Vince Guaraldi
Arranged by Carolyn Miller

Moderately

Linus and Lucy

By Vince Guaraldi
Arranged by Carolyn Miller

Play both hands one octave higher when performing as a duet.

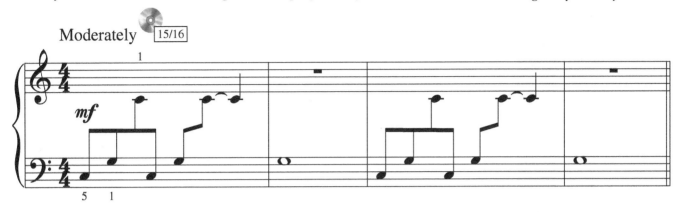

28

Optional Teacher Accompaniment

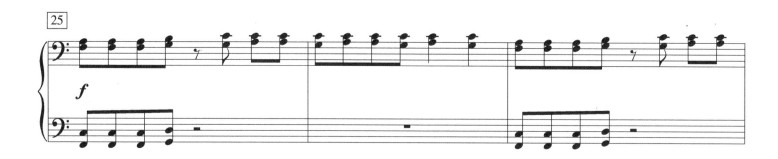

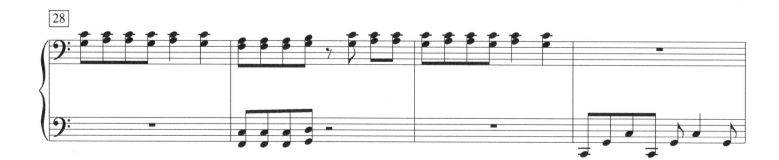

poco rit.

poco rit.

The Muppet Show Theme

Optional Teacher Accompaniment

Words and Music by Jim Henson
and Sam Pottle
Arranged by Carolyn Miller

Joyfully

The Muppet Show Theme

Words and Music by Jim Henson
and Sam Pottle
Arranged by Carolyn Miller

Play both hands one octave higher when performing as a duet.

Optional Teacher Accompaniment

real - ly makes me hap - py to in - tro - duce to you.

It's time to put on make - up. It's time to dress up right.

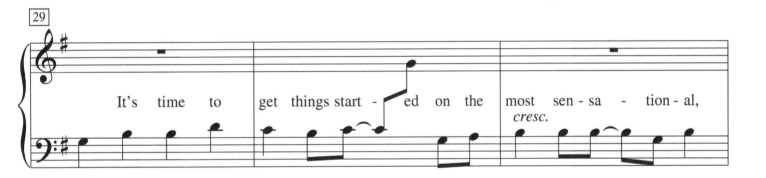

It's time to get things start - ed on the most sen - sa - tion - al,

in - spi - ra - tion - al, cel - e - bra - tion - al, mup - pet - a - tion - al. This is what we

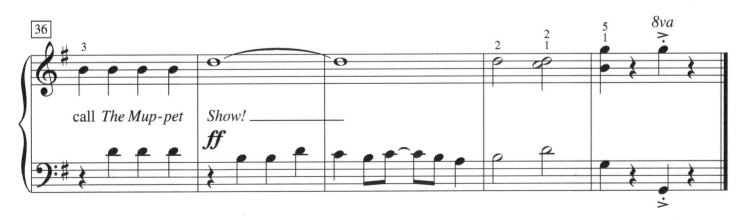

call *The Mup-pet Show!*

Sesame Street Theme

Optional Teacher Accompaniment

Words by Bruce Hart, Jon Stone and Joe Raposo
Music by Joe Raposo
Arranged by Carolyn Miller

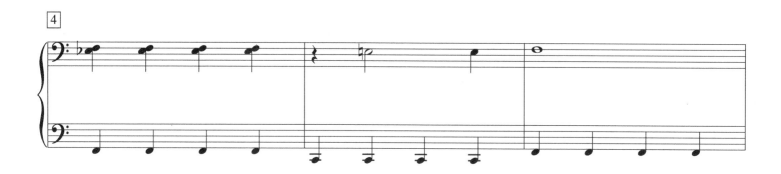

Sesame Street Theme

Words by Bruce Hart, Jon Stone and Joe Raposo
Music by Joe Raposo
Arranged by Carolyn Miller

Play both hands one octave higher when performing as a duet.

Optional Teacher Accompaniment

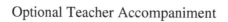

Spectacular Piano Solos
from

WILLIS MUSIC

www.willispianomusic.com

Early Elementary

00416850	Barnyard Strut/*Glenda Austin*	$2.99
00416702	Big Green Frog/*Carolyn C. Setliff*	$2.99
00416904	The Blizzard/*Glenda Austin*	$2.99
00416882	Bow-Wow Blues/*Glenda Austin*	$2.99
00416883	Catch Me!/*Frank Levin*	$2.99
00406670	Cookies/*Carolyn Miller*	$2.95
00404218	Fog at Sea/*William Gillock*	$2.95
00416907	Guardian Angels/*Naoko Ikeda*	$2.99
00416918	Halloween Surprise/*Ronald Bennett*	$2.99
00412099	Moccasin Dance/*John Thompson*	$1.95
00416783	My Missing Teeth/*Carolyn C. Setliff*	$2.95
00416933	The Perceptive Detective/*Carolyn Miller*	$2.99
00416816	Rain, Rain/*Carolyn Miller*	$2.99

Mid-Elementary

00416780	The Acrobat/*Carolyn Miller*	$2.99
00416041	Autumn Is Here/*William Gillock*	$2.99
00416902	Cherokee Prayer of Peace/*Glenda Austin*	$2.99
00416803	The Dancing Bears/*Carolyn Miller*	$2.99
00416878	Mini Toccata/*Eric Baumgartner*	$2.99
00416958	Miss Kitty Kat/*Glenda Austin*	$2.99
00404738	Moonlight/*William Gillock*	$2.95
00416872	The Rainbow/*Carolyn Miller*	$2.99
00416728	Seahorse Serenade/*Carolyn C. Setliff*	$2.95
00416674	Seaside Dancer/*Ronald Bennett*	$2.50
00416785	Watermelon Sunset/*Randall Hartsell*	$2.95

Later Elementary

00416840	At the Ballet/*Carolyn C. Setliff*	$2.99
00416852	Black Cat Chat/*Eric Baumgartner*	$2.99
00416887	Chromatic Craze/*Carolyn C. Setliff*	$2.99
00416786	Egyptian Journey/*Randall Hartsell*	$2.95
00416906	Evening Melody/*Naoko Ikeda*	$2.99
00416886	Flying Fingers/*Carolyn C. Setliff*	$2.99
00416836	The Gentle Brook/*Carolyn Miller*	$2.99
00416908	The Goblins Gather/*Frank Levin*	$2.99
00405918	Monkey on a Stick/*Lynn Freeman Olson*	$2.95
00416866	October Leaves/*Carolyn C. Setliff*	$2.99
00406552	Parisian Waltz/*Robert Donahue*	$2.95
00416781	The Race Car/*Carolyn Miller*	$2.95
00416885	Scaling the Peaks/*Randall Hartsell*	$2.99
00406564	Showdown/*Ronald Bennett*	$2.95
00416919	Sparkling Waterfall/*Carolyn C. Setliff*	$2.99
00416820	Star Wonders/*Randall Hartsell*	$2.99
00416779	Sunrise at San Miguel/*Ronald Bennett*	$2.99
00416828	Tick Tock/*Eric Baumgartner*	$2.99
00416881	Twilight Tarantella/*Glenda Austin*	$2.99

Early Intermediate

00416943	Autumn Nocturne/*Susan Alcon*	$2.99
00405455	Bass Train Boogie/*Stephen Adoff*	$2.99
00416817	Broken Arm Blues/*Carolyn Miller*	$2.99
00416841	The Bubbling Brook/*Carolyn Miller*	$2.99
00416849	Bye-Bye Blues/*Glenda Austin*	$2.99
00416945	Cafe Francais/*Jonathan Maiocco*	$2.99
00416834	Canopy of Stars/*Randall Hartsell*	$2.99
00416956	Dancing in a Dream/*William Gillock*	$2.99
00415585	Flamenco/*William Gillock*	$2.95
00416856	Garden of Dreams/*Naoko Ikeda*	$2.99
00416818	Majestic Splendor/*Carolyn C. Setliff*	$2.99
00416948	Manhattan Swing/*Naoko Ikeda*	$2.99

00416733	The Matador/*Carolyn Miller*	$2.99
00416940	Medieval Rondo/*Carolyn C. Setliff*	$2.99
00416942	A Melancholy Night/*Naoko Ikeda*	$2.99
00416877	Mystic Quest/*Randall Hartsell*	$2.99
00416873	Le Papillon (The Butterfly)/*Glenda Austin*	$2.99
00416829	Scherzo Nuovo/*Eric Baumgartner*	$2.99
00416947	Snowflakes in Spring/*Naoko Ikeda*	$2.99
00416937	Stampede/*Carolyn Miller*	$2.99
00416917	Supernova/*Ronald Bennett*	$2.99
00416842	Tarantella in G Minor/*Glenda Austin*	$2.99
00416782	Toccata Caprice/*Carolyn C. Setliff*	$2.95
00416938	Toccatina Tag/*Ronald Bennett*	$2.99
00416869	Twilight Tapestry/*Randall Hartsell*	$2.99
00416924	A Waltz to Remember/*Glenda Austin*	$2.99

Mid-Intermediate

00416848	American Syncopations/*Eric Baumgartner*	$3.99
00416698	Black Key Blues/*Alexander Peskanov*	$2.95
00416911	Blues Streak/*Eric Baumgartner*	$2.99
00416855	Dance of the Unicorn/*Naoko Ikeda*	$2.99
00416893	Fantasia in A Minor/*Randall Hartsell*	$2.99
00416821	Foggy Blues/*Naoko Ikeda*	$2.99
00414908	Fountain in the Rain/*William Gillock*	$2.99
00416765	Grand Sonatina in G/*Glenda Austin*	$2.95
00416875	Himalayan Grandeur/*Randall Hartsell*	$2.99
00406630	Jazz Suite No. 2/*Glenda Austin*	$3.95
00416910	Little Rock (& Roll)/*Eric Baumgartner*	$2.99
00416939	Midnight Fantasy/*Carolyn C. Setliff*	$2.99
00416857	Moonlight Rose/*Naoko Ikeda*	$2.99
00414627	Portrait of Paris/*William Gillock*	$2.99
00405171	Sea Nocturne/*Glenda Austin*	$2.99
00416844	Sea Tempest/*Randall Hartsell*	$2.99
00415517	Sonatine/*William Gillock*	$2.99
00416701	Spanish Romance/*arr. Frank Levin*	$2.95
00416946	Stormy Seas/*Carolyn Miller*	$2.99
00416100	Three Jazz Preludes/*William Gillock*	$3.95

Later Intermediate

00416715	Hear the Spirit of America/*Marilyn Briant and Andrew Zatman*	$2.95
00416764	Romantic Rhapsody/*Glenda Austin*	$2.95
00405646	Soft Lights/*Carolyn Jones Campbell*	$1.95
00409464	Tarantella/*A. Pieczonka*	$2.95

Early Advanced

00415263	Impromptu/*Mildred T. Souers*	$2.95
00415166	Sleighbells in the Snow/*William Gillock*	$2.95
00405264	Valse Brillante/*Glenda Austin*	$2.95

HAL•LEONARD® CORPORATION

7777 W. BLUEMOUND RD. P.O. BOX 13819 MILWAUKEE, WI 53213

CLOSER LOOK View sample pages and hear audio excerpts online at www.halleonard.com

www.facebook.com/willispianomusic

Prices & availability subject to change without notice.

0412

TEACHING LITTLE FINGERS TO PLAY MORE

TEACHING LITTLE FINGERS TO PLAY MORE
by Leigh Kaplan
Teaching Little Fingers to Play More is a fun-filled and colorfully illustrated follow-up book to *Teaching Little Fingers to Play*. It strengthens skills learned while carefully easing the transition into John Thompson's *Modern Course, First Grade*.
00406137 Book only $6.99
00406527 Book/Audio $9.99

SUPPLEMENTARY SERIES
All books include optional teacher accompaniments.

BROADWAY SONGS
arr. Carolyn Miller
MID TO LATER ELEMENTARY LEVEL
10 great show tunes for students to enjoy, including: Edelweiss • I Whistle a Happy Tune • I Won't Grow Up • Maybe • The Music of the Night • and more.
00416928 Book only $6.99
00416929 Book/Audio $12.99

CHILDREN'S SONGS
arr. Carolyn Miller
MID-ELEMENTARY LEVEL
10 songs: The Candy Man • Do-Re-Mi • I'm Popeye the Sailor Man • It's a Small World • Linus and Lucy • The Muppet Show Theme • Sesame Street Theme • Supercalifragilisticexpialidocious • Tomorrow.
00416810 Book only $6.99
00416811 Book/Audio $12.99

CLASSICS
arr. Randall Hartsell
MID-ELEMENTARY LEVEL
7 solos: Marche Slave • Over the Waves • Polovtsian Dance (from the opera *Prince Igor*) • Pomp and Circumstance • Rondeau • Waltz (from the ballet *Sleeping Beauty*) • William Tell Overture.
00406760 Book only $5.99
00416513 Book/Audio $10.99

DISNEY TUNES
arr. Glenda Austin
MID-ELEMENTARY LEVEL
9 songs, including: Circle of Life • Colors of the Wind • A Dream Is a Wish Your Heart Makes • A Spoonful of Sugar • Under the Sea • A Whole New World • and more.
00416750 Book only $9.99
00416751 Book/Audio $12.99

EASY DUETS
arr. Carolyn Miller
MID-ELEMENTARY LEVEL
9 equal-level duets: A Bicycle Built for Two • Blow the Man Down • Chopsticks • Do Your Ears Hang Low? • I've Been Working on the Railroad • The Man on the Flying Trapeze • Short'nin' Bread • Skip to My Lou • The Yellow Rose of Texas.
00416832 Book only $6.99
00416833 Book/Audio $10.99

JAZZ AND ROCK
Eric Baumgartner
MID-ELEMENTARY LEVEL
11 solos, including: Big Bass Boogie • Crescendo Rock • Funky Fingers • Jazz Waltz in G • Rockin' Rhythm • Squirrel Race • and more!
00406765 Book only $5.99

MOVIE MUSIC
arr. Carolyn Miller
LATER ELEMENTARY LEVEL
10 magical movie arrangements: Bella's Lullaby (Twilight) • Somewhere Out There (An American Tail) • True Love's Kiss (Enchanted) • and more.
00139190 Book/Audio $10.99

Also available:

AMERICAN TUNES
arr. Eric Baumgartner
MID-ELEMENTARY LEVEL
00406755 Book only $6.99

BLUES AND BOOGIE
Carolyn Miller
MID-ELEMENTARY LEVEL
00406764 Book only $5.99

CHRISTMAS CAROLS
arr. Carolyn Miller
MID-ELEMENTARY LEVEL
00406763 Book only $6.99

CHRISTMAS CLASSICS
arr. Eric Baumgartner
MID-ELEMENTARY LEVEL
00416827 Book only $6.99
00416826 Book/Audio $12.99

CHRISTMAS FAVORITES
arr. Eric Baumgartner
MID-ELEMENTARY LEVEL
00416723 Book only $7.99
00416724 Book/Audio $12.99

FAMILIAR TUNES
arr. Glenda Austin
MID-ELEMENTARY LEVEL
00406761 Book only $6.99

HYMNS
arr. Glenda Austin
MID-ELEMENTARY LEVEL
00406762 Book only $6.99

JEWISH FAVORITES
arr. Eric Baumgartner
MID-ELEMENTARY LEVEL
00416755 Book only $5.99

RECITAL PIECES
Carolyn Miller
MID-ELEMENTARY LEVEL
00416540 Book only $5.99

SONGS FROM MANY LANDS
arr. Carolyn C. Setliff
MID-ELEMENTARY LEVEL
00416688 Book only $5.99

EXCLUSIVELY DISTRIBUTED BY

WILLIS MUSIC

HAL•LEONARD®

Complete song lists online at
www.halleonard.com